Bess of Hardwick

Jill Armitage

BRADWELL
BOOKS

Published by Bradwell Books

9 Orgreave Close Sheffield S13 9NP

books@bradwellbooks.co.uk

British Library Cataloguing in Publication Data: a catalogue record for this book is available from the British Library.

1st Edition

ISBN: 9781912060627

Design by: Mark Titterton

Text by: Jill Armitage

Photography: The author and credited individually

Print: Gomer Press, Llandysul, Ceredigion SA44 4JL

Cover image: Countess of Shrewsbury. ©National Trust

Contents

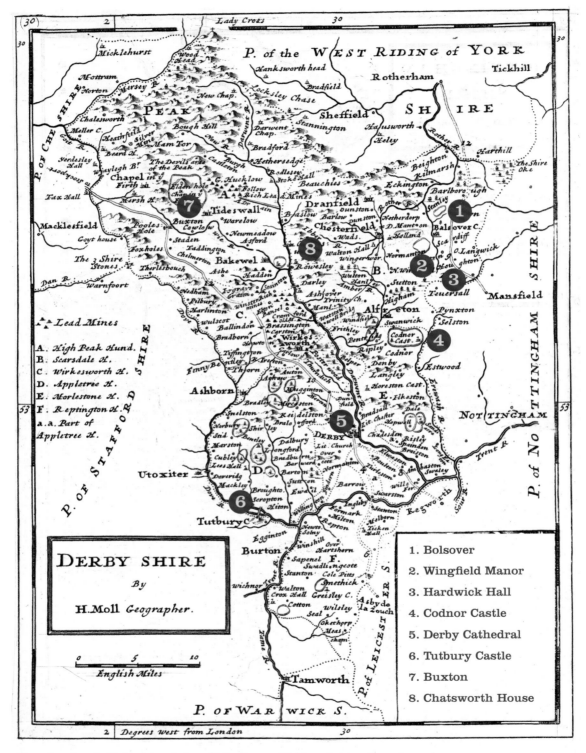

Map reproduced with kind permission of Miss Frances Webb and picturethepast.org.uk

Introduction

As you drive along the Derbyshire stretch of the M1 motorway look east, where side by side, dominating the remote skyline, stand two halls. One is the remodelled – though now ruinous – family home of the Hardwick family, who by the fifteenth century had been established there for at least six generations. The other is the magnificent Hardwick Hall, closely connected in popular imagination with one person: Bess, the ambitious daughter of the Hardwick family who rose to become the redoubtable Elizabeth, Countess of Shrewsbury.

As the light reflects off the many-faceted windows of Hardwick Hall, it looks like a huge lantern, topped with her initials – ES – and her coat of arms. Both halls and their predecessor, the great Chatsworth House, are outstanding statements of the determination, wealth and power of a local squire's daughter who rose to be one of the richest and most remarkable women of Elizabethan England. The driving force of her life was to found a dynasty and in this she succeeded. As Horace Walpole wrote in 1760:

> When Hardwick's Towers shall bow their head
> Nor mass be more in Worksop said
> When Bolsover's fair fame shall tend
> Like Oldcotes, to its smouldering end
> When Chatsworth tastes no Ca'endish bounties
> Let fame forget this costly countess.

Bess was also responsible for building Oldcotes, now demolished; Bolsover Castle and Worksop Manor were Cavendish/Shrewsbury properties.

Hardwick Hall.

Barry Skeates Creative Commons

1 Bess's Early Years and a Widow at Sixteen

Bess of Hardwick was born in 1527 into the relative obscurity of small gentry whose ancestors had been established at Hardwick on the Derbyshire/Nottinghamshire border for at least six generations. Hardwick means sheep farm, a clue to the hilly, wooded pastureland from which it originates. John Hardwick married Elizabeth Leake of Hasland, and although there is no actual record of their birthdates, Elizabeth gave birth to four daughters and a son before the birth of Elizabeth, better known as Bess. Within weeks Elizabeth Hardwick was again pregnant but John Hardwick became gravely ill. Before he died on 29 January 1528, he tried to make provision for his young family and nominated eight trustees to hold the land, which was to be administrated for the benefit of his widow and children for twenty years, by which time the eighteen-month-old James would be twenty-one and could inherit. John's will provided '40 marks of good and lawful money' for each of his daughters at the time of their marriages and an allowance for his unborn child.

The Hardwick estate was well established but, despite John's efforts, the Crown took control of the land, leaving his widow with no income or financial support. Elizabeth and her young family were allowed to remain in their home but had to pay for the privilege. Young James was taken into wardship, and there's a possibility that the four girls were sent to live with relatives, although there's no record to confirm this.

Their situation was financial turmoil, so Elizabeth did what most widows and widowers of the day did: she remarried. Her second husband was Ralph Leche, a younger son of another local gentry family who owned an estate at Chatsworth. He had no expectations, but a few leases that brought in an annuity of just £6.13s 4d (£6.66) a year. The birth of three more daughters did nothing to mitigate their circumstances. Between 1538 and 1544, Ralph Leche was imprisoned in the Fleet Prison London for debt, and in 1545 he was committed to debtor's prison in Derby.

The situation was probably eased when fifteen-year-old Mary Hardwick was betrothed to Richard Wingfield, Esq. of Crowfield, Suffolk, Jane Hardwick was betrothed to Godfrey Boswell of Penistone, South Yorkshire and ten-year-old Alice to Francis Leche, son of her stepfather's eldest brother. In 1538, eleven-year-old Bess was sent to the great household of a distant cousin, Sir George and Lady Zouche of Codnor Castle. This is where she met Robert Barlow, a young gentleman from a neighbouring gentry family also in service in the Zouche household.

Codnor Castle

Robert Barlow was the eldest son and heir of Arthur Barlow, who owned estates on the Derbyshire/Yorkshire border. Arthur Barlow had become gravely ill, but before he died on 28 May 1543 he tried to make provision for his family by arranging a marriage between his thirteen-year-old son Robert and fifteen-year-old Bess. The marriage took place in the spring of 1543 but because of their young age, there is no evidence that they lived together as man and wife. Bess's marriage would have given her a new measure of respect and she probably moved in with Robert and his widowed mother and made her home at Barlow Woodseats Hall.

However, soon afterwards Robert became ill and died on Christmas Eve 1544. The young widow was just sixteen and very likely to have still been a virgin but the law entitled her to a widow's portion of her late husband's estate. The Barlow family refused and Bess spent two years fighting for her rights. Eventually she became the life tenant of a third of the manor of Barlow, with all the land and properties that entailed, giving her a dower pension of about £30 a year, around £1,500 in today's currency.

This gave Bess independence, and an opportunity to better herself. She gained a position in the household of Lady Frances Grey, wife of Henry Grey, 3rd Marquess of Dorset, and their daughters Jane, Katherine and Mary Grey. Lady Frances was granddaughter of Henry VII, daughter of Mary Tudor, niece of Henry VIII and cousin to Edward, Mary and Elizabeth. Bess Barlow was about to be introduced into the top strata of Tudor society.

2 Bess Becomes Lady Cavendish

The Grey family home was Bradgate House in Leicestershire and it was there that Bess met and married Sir William Cavendish in 1547. He was aged forty, to Bess's nineteen years. Sir William recorded in his notebook – *'Memorandum. That I was married unto Elizabeth Hardwicke my third wife in Leestersheer at Bradgate House, the 20th August in the first year of King Edward's reign, at two of the clock after midnight.'* The time of the wedding, in the early hours of the morning, had been carefully calculated to fit favourable astrological predictions. Bess was very superstitious about such things and later she had an astrologer in her household.

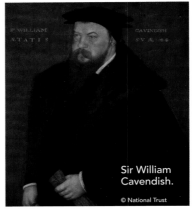

Sir William Cavendish.

© National Trust

The second son of a Suffolk squire, Sir William had become a commissioner for the dissolution of the monasteries under Henry VIII, and had been awarded many former monastic properties and land. In 1546 he received a knighthood, become a Privy Councillor, and was appointed Treasurer of the King's Chamber, a position which he bought for £1,000. In possession of great energy and ability, he was a businessman, a speculator and a profiteer. What Bess brought to the marriage was pragmatism, prudence and rigour, and despite their age difference they were very well suited.

One of the former monastic manors, Northaw in Hertfordshire, became their main home but they divided their time between there and their London house in the shadow of St Paul's Cathedral. Two of the children from Sir William's first marriage lived with them and within ten years Bess had

produced another eight children, two of whom died in infancy. In 1548 she gave birth to Frances, named after her friend Lady Frances Grey. The following year Lady Jane Grey was godmother to Bess's daughter Temperance, who sadly lived for only a short time. Henry, their son and heir, was born the following year and his godmother was the young Princess Elizabeth.

Lady Frances Grey

It was around this time that Francis Leche, who had married Bess's younger sister Alice, decided to sell his Chatsworth estate and Sir William was persuaded by Bess to buy it for £6,000. The following year, they pursued a determined programme of buying up land surrounding the estate.

A deal was made with the Crown whereby Sir William's Hertfordshire estates, including Northaw, were exchanged for Derbyshire land at Doveridge. The manor of Ashford together with 8,000 acres was purchased from the Earl of Westmoreland, and other smaller parcels of land were also obtained. These were all cannily bought in the joint names of William and Bess. This made sound business sense because in the event of William's death, and with Henry, his heir, being underage, Bess would be in control, not the Court of Wards.

Two more sons followed – William born in 1551 and Charles in 1553 – then came three daughters, Elizabeth in 1555, Mary in 1556, and Lucretia who was born and died in 1557. By this time, the Cavendish family occupied a more imposing house in London, but with her growing family and so much land and property in Derbyshire, the Cavendish family wanted a suitable home there too.

Bradgate House as it stands today, showing the outer walls and parts of the old building.
Creative Commons

3 Bess Builds Chatsworth House

Bess embarked on her first major building project, to revamp the existing Chatsworth House which was in a poor state of repair. But she wasn't content to simply alter, she wanted to build, and in 1551 a mason named Roger Worth was paid to draw up plans for a new Chatsworth House. To replace the dilapidated manor house, they planned to erect an extremely large, quadrangular and sumptuously furnished house. Building work began but stopped abruptly when Sir William died on 25 October 1557. After ten years of marriage, Bess found herself once again a widow, with six children, two stepchildren, a half-finished Chatsworth House and many debts.

A deficit had been found in Sir William's treasury accounts. Someone had to be accountable and, because Sir William was dead, his widow Bess was stuck with the debt. The obvious answer was to sell Chatsworth and all the land, but that wasn't an option for Bess. In 1558, when Elizabeth became queen, Bess was appointed a lady-in-waiting and went to live at court. This not only provided her with accommodation in London while fighting the many lawsuits pertaining to the debts left by Sir William, but it also offered unrivalled opportunities to mix with all the influential people of the realm – and indeed for husband hunting. That's how she met Sir William St Loe, a widower with large tracts of land in Somerset and Gloucestershire. As Captain of the Guard and Chief Butler of England he enjoyed a comfortable income of £500 a year.

A Tudor engraving of Chatsworth House

Bess Cavendish and William St Loe were married in the autumn of 1559. He promised not just to support her, her children and stepchildren, but also to settle the outstanding debt left by William Cavendish, and pay for the building of Chatsworth to continue. Bess now divided her time between London and Chatsworth, but because of his court duties St Loe lived mainly in London. The enforced separation came to an end when Bess was appointed a Lady of the Queen's Bedchamber, one of the most prestigious positions in the court. She took her place in the intimate circle at court and no doubt witnessed at first hand the Queen's love affair with Robert Dudley.

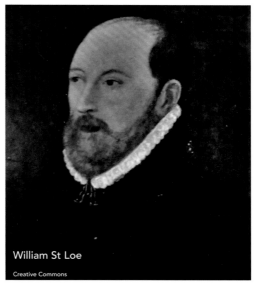

William St Loe

Creative Commons

While in London Bess used her time well, buying luxury items for Chatsworth and arranging a marriage for her eldest daughter Frances to Henry Pierrepont. But William St Loe's health was causing concern and his brother Edward was spreading rumours that Bess was poisoning him. These charges not only infuriated William St Loe, they even prompted him to change his will in Bess's favour so that when he died, at the end of 1564, Bess became a very wealthy widow.

Not only was she in possession of all the Derbyshire land acquired through her first widow's dowry and the estates she had bought with her second husband William Cavendish, she also had all William St Loe's lands in Somerset and Gloucestershire, which altogether gave her an annual income of £1,600. These assets considerably upped her desirability in the marriage market and soon rumours were circulating as to who would be husband number four. Now thirty-eight, Bess was a physically attractive woman and there was no shortage of suitors for her hand.

4 Bess Becomes Countess of Shrewsbury

Before long, one of the richest men in England made her a proposal. He was George Talbot, 6th Earl of Shrewsbury, commander of the armies of the north, Lord Lieutenant of Yorkshire, Derbyshire and Nottinghamshire, and Chamberlain of the Exchequer. His wealth was securely founded on ancestral estates, and on the profitable mines and industries of Sheffield, whose castle was his principle seat. He also owned vast expanses of land in Derbyshire, Nottinghamshire, Shropshire, Staffordshire and Yorkshire with castles and manor houses which included Sheffield Manor and Castle, Wingfield Manor, Worksop Manor, Buxton Hall, Welbeck Abbey and Rufford Abbey, together with leases from the Crown, among which were Tutbury Castle and Abbey in Staffordshire. There were also at least four properties in London to add to this impressive list.

George Talbot, 6th Earl of Shrewsbury

A portrait of George Talbot in his prime shows a commanding figure with a serious expression, but he was considered to be a joyless man. George and Bess were of the same age, with children from previous marriages, and when they married in 1567 it was in what amounted to a triple ceremony. Bess married the Earl and officially became the Countess of Shrewsbury, her eldest son and heir, Henry Cavendish, then aged seventeen, married the Earl's eight-year-old daughter Grace Talbot, and the Earl's second son, sixteen-year-old Gilbert Talbot, married Bess's youngest daughter, twelve-year-old Mary Cavendish. This was not unusual in influential families. It was an effective way to ensure a powerful dynasty, and Bess was determined to form one of the strongest in the land.

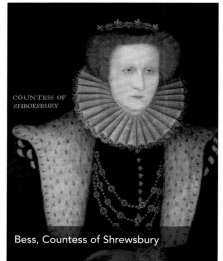

COUNTESS OF SHROESBURY

Bess, Countess of Shrewsbury

As a three-times widow, Bess had her own considerable wealth, land and property, but as a married woman this was all taken by her husband. A married woman had to give up all her financial independence, and in marrying Bess, George Talbot, Earl of Shrewsbury, gained full control of her lands. However, she had a clause written into their marriage settlement that, in exchange for giving all her land, property and wealth to Shrewsbury, one third of his unsettled income would go to Bess on his death. She also made certain stipulations about Chatsworth to ensure that it would pass to her eldest son and heir Henry Cavendish on her death. Marriage in the upper society of sixteenth-century England was very much a business arrangement and the combined wealth of the Cavendish and Shrewsbury families from properties, land holdings, mineral rights and farming was enormous.

The marriage was off to a good start and in surviving correspondence from Shrewsbury to Bess, he addresses her affectionately as 'my none' (my own), 'my own sweetheart' and 'my own dear heart'. Bess no longer attended court and the queen sent a message saying: *'I have been glad to see my Lady St Loe, but am I now more desirous to see my Lady Shrewsbury. I hope my Lady hath known my good opinion of her … I assure you there is no Lady in this land that I better love and like.'*

Looking over Paine's Bridge with Chatsworth House in the distance

iStock

15

5 The Shrewsburys Become Mary, Queen of Scots' Jailers

In autumn 1568, Shrewsbury was summoned to London by Queen Elizabeth and there he was informed that he and Bess had been chosen as the custodians of Mary, Queen of Scots, who had fled to England after being imprisoned in Scotland under suspicion of murdering her husband Henry Darnley. Shrewsbury considered it a rare honour and was undoubtedly flattered as *'the queen did trust him as she did few'*, but this turned out to be a doubtful privilege.

Portrait of Mary, Queen of Scots and Darnley

© National Trust Images/

They were told to receive their royal captive at Tutbury Castle, where she was to be lodged until it was decided what to do with her. The fact that Tutbury Castle was not a residence in a fit state to receive a queen seemed immaterial. It was an old motte-and-bailey castle built after the Norman conquest of 1066. Patched up and altered over the centuries, the castle had in parts fallen into ruin, the roofs leaked and the walls were crumbling. The ancient structure was built beside a marsh from which malodorous fumes arose, the middens stank and the draughts and winds whistled through the chambers. It was used only occasionally as a hunting lodge so furniture was sparse, but Queen Elizabeth paid no heed to this. Her main concern was that it

Queen Elizabeth I

© National Trust Images/John Hammond

was remote and fortified. Despite Shrewsbury's concerns and request for a more suitable place to be found for the Scottish Queen, he was met with a wall of silence and secrecy that lasted for months. Then, on 20 January, Bess received a letter from the Earl of Leicester instructing her to prepare Tutbury for the queen's arrival on 3 February.

Just a year after their marriage, the Earl and Countess of Shrewsbury became the custodians of Mary, Queen of Scots, an arduous and financially onerous task. Her household was supposed to consist of thirty people but had risen to over sixty, so playing host to the captive queen was, for the Shrewsburys, rather like running a small hotel. The honour of being appointed jailer to a spoilt royal captive was outweighed by practical considerations and obligations.

Tutbury Castle
Duncan Harris Creative Commons

Throughout the whole period of her imprisonment, Mary steadfastly refused to make any financial contribution, although as the widow of Francis II of France she had a dowager's pension of £12,000 annually which she continued to use to finance her plans for escape. She insisted that her imprisonment was illegal and she was therefore justified in taking advantage of any means to secure her liberty.

Understandably, after each plot was foiled security had to be stepped up with a corresponding rise in costs to be met by the Shrewsburys. The seventeenth-century biographer Johnston estimated that it was costing them £30 a day or £10,000 a year to keep Mary and her household, yet Queen Elizabeth paid only £52 a week, a quarter of the amount.

The Shrewsburys treated Mary with unfailing courtesy and consideration, aware that one day she might be Queen of England, and in the early days of her captivity Bess had a very good relationship with her. Despite their twenty-year age difference, they were both gifted needlewomen and spent time together embroidering in Bess's own chamber. Keeping Queen Elizabeth informed of events, in March 1569 Shrewsbury wrote: *'The queen continueth daily resort into my wife's chamber where she sits working with the needle. They talk together of indifferent trifling matters, without any sign of secret dealing or practice.'*

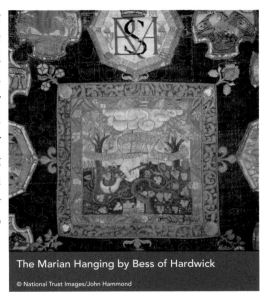

The Marian Hanging by Bess of Hardwick
© National Trust Images/John Hammond

It was during their early years together that the joint embroideries attributed to them at Hardwick Hall, Derbyshire, Oxburgh Hall, Norfolk and elsewhere were completed. But hidden inside the parcels of silks and sewing materials sent to Mary there were often concealed notes from her Catholic sympathisers, who were constantly plotting on her behalf. There were frequent plots to free Mary, and when it was discovered that Mary was participating fully in escape plans, she was unrepentant.

Normally the extended Shrewsbury household would move to another of their properties after two months, using the houses in a system of rotation, to allow the buildings to be thoroughly cleaned for health reasons. Exacerbated by the foul conditions at Tutbury, Mary's health had become a matter of concern. She was in the habit of fainting and complained of a constant pain in her side, then developed a fever.

Getting Queen Elizabeth's permission to move the chronically sick Mary Stuart from Tutbury Castle to South Wingfield Manor was comparatively easy when compared to the actual transfer, which took place on 20 April 1569. It was a major operation transporting the Scottish Queen and her mini court, which by now had grown to one hundred people, the twenty-six miles from Tutbury to South Wingfield. The move was financed by Shrewsbury, and assured of security by the assistance of the local justices of the county, but the change of location did not help Mary's condition and her health continued to decline as she was moved between Chatsworth House, South Wingfield Manor and Tutbury Castle.

Queen Marys Bower, Chatsworth
Creative Commons

Bess and Mary would have spent many hours together, playing the lute, working on embroidery and dressmaking. Their companionship at this time included swapping stories and gossip. Mary's life had been a full one and no doubt Bess, who had never ventured outside England, showed a keen interest in French court life. The two ladies undoubtedly talked freely about their different lives at the French and English courts, sharing a few stories of indiscretions, something that Bess would bitterly regret years later when Mary used this knowledge against her.

When Shrewsbury suffered a slight stroke, Bess took him to Buxton to take the curative waters but the furious Queen Elizabeth ordered them to return immediately to Tutbury to guard their prisoner. With her freedom curtailed, Bess must have felt almost as restrained as the captive queen. Their carefree lifestyle was over. Keeping their expensive royal prisoner and her entourage was a full-time chore and an uncalled for, burdensome strain for them. They were committed twenty-four hours a day, every day. They could never relax. Their lives were constantly disturbed by the intrigues of the captive queen and the suspicions of the reigning one.

Having a permanent house guest of royal rank meant that, on the English Queen's orders, they could no longer entertain, so they were cut off from their friends and family, and now they were being told to curtail all their outside activities too. No wonder the good relationship between Bess and Mary was wearing very thin.

Another of Mary's prisons was Sheffield Manor, on the eastern side of the city of Sheffield. With a boundary fence of about eight miles, it enclosed one of the largest deer parks in England. The Manor was built in 1516 by the 4th Earl of Shrewsbury to replace Sheffield Castle, a fortified castle built in 1270 upon a steep-sided sandstone outcrop overlooking the confluence of the Rivers Don and Sheaf. It was one of the largest castles in medieval England but by the sixteenth century it was

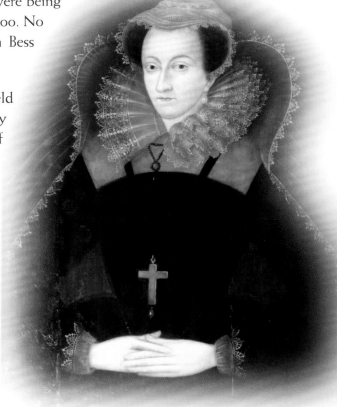

Right: Mary, Queen of Scots aged 42

© National Trust / Simon Harris

The Old Hall Hotel, Buxton

Mark Titterton

antiquated and out of date. However, because the short distance from Sheffield Castle to Sheffield Manor meant that it was much easier to move the captive queen between them when cleaning was necessary, they became her base for many years.

There are few of Mary's many letters written over the next fifteen years in which she doesn't refer to the constant pain she had to suffer. Her digestive upsets, stiffness, aching limbs and the pain in her side which plagued her all her life were interspersed with bouts of severe illness which on several occasions became critical and almost proved fatal. Acute pains in her arms which prevented her from writing, attacks of fever and the gradual onset of rheumatism aggravated by the dampness of some of her prisons took their toll on Mary Stuart.

Bess, who had always enjoyed robust health, probably lost all patience, particularly when Shrewsbury, who suffered occasionally from bouts of painful ill health due to his gout, came down with 'the hot ague'. As his recovery was slow, Bess wrote to Elizabeth asking for permission to accompany him to Buxton to take the curative waters. When she received no reply they went ahead with the journey anyway, then faced the queen's wrath.

In 1572, the entrepreneurial Shrewsburys saw an opportunity to build an impressive new bath house in the centre of Buxton on the foundations of an earlier inn or hostelry where the warm springs surfaced. They installed a fashionable doctor named John Jones, who declared that the thermal waters were efficacious for almost every ill of the human body. Understandably this attracted great fame, and a wealthy, aristocratic clientele who flocked to take advantage of the curative, beneficial properties of the healing water. Buxton became a fashionable spa town and an elegant place in which to spend time.

The Hot Baths, Buxton.

After another stay at Tutbury, where Mary's health continued to cause concern, on 10 August 1573 the Queen eventually gave her consent for Mary to visit Buxton to take the waters to seek relief from her chronic arthritis. It was the first of six visits Mary was to make to the Derbyshire spa town between 1573 and 1583, but tight restrictions were placed on her liberty there.

6 Marital Discord Between the Shrewsburys

In the autumn of 1574, Mary, Queen of Scots' mother-in-law, the Countess of Lennox, set off from London to visit her estates in the north of England, accompanied by her nineteen-year-old son Charles Stuart. Permission had been granted provided that she did not make contact with her daughter-in-law, but on the way Bess invited them to break their journey at Rufford Abbey, another of the Shrewsbury seats that lay just off the Great North Road. Bess and her nineteen-year-old unmarried daughter Elizabeth Cavendish were there to welcome them and, by a strange coincidence, the Countess of Lennox became indisposed. Bess occupied herself looking after the invalid while a love affair developed between Elizabeth Cavendish and Charles Stuart. The result, in the Countess of Lennox's words, was that *'Charles entangled himself so that he would have no other'* and a speedy marriage was arranged. Because Charles Stuart was of royal blood, permission should have been sought from the Queen but it wasn't, and when she heard she ordered the two countesses and the newlyweds down to London where they were placed under house arrest. The Countess of Lennox was sent to the Tower, but it's hardly likely that Bess would have shared her fate when she was responsible for the care of the captive Queen of Scots back in Derbyshire.

Elizabeth Cavendish/Lennox gave birth to a daughter named Arbella, but the following year Charles Stuart died and the Lennox title and land was seized.

The Countess of Lennox had expected to acquire a hefty sum of dowry money from the Cavendish/Shrewsburys, but Shrewsbury, who controlled the finances, refused to pay anything. Bess pleaded with Shrewsbury to give her daughter what was rightfully hers but Shrewsbury maintained that because the marriage took place without his approval, he would give her nothing. When the Countess of Lennox died in mysterious circumstances, without her rightful marriage dowry, the widowed Elizabeth and Arbella were destitute and in December 1578 they returned to the family home at Chatsworth. Originally Queen Elizabeth wanted to ensure they didn't share the same roof as the imprisoned Scottish queen but when this became impractical, she reluctantly changed her mind.

Things were no longer quite so harmonious between Bess and Shrewsbury. Not only was he not prepared to honour the agreements drawn up by him and Bess in their 1567 marriage contract to provide a dowry for Elizabeth, he was also refusing to give £20,000 to each of Bess's sons when they reached the age of twenty-one. Shrewsbury always managed to wriggle out of parting with money where Bess was concerned, and although Bess had brought great wealth to the marriage, she had no say on how her money was spent. Bess would have

Lady Arabella Stuart aged 23 months

© National Trust Images/John Hammond

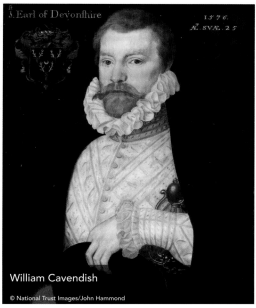

William Cavendish

© National Trust Images/John Hammond

provided Elizabeth's dowry herself, but the law dictated that a married woman could have no independent finances, a situation that was bound to cause a lot of friction between Bess and her husband.

Things were perhaps brought to a head when Bess's brother James Hardwick, who had inherited the Hardwick estate that had been Bess's childhood home, was declared bankrupt and thrown into debtor's prison. Bess asked Shrewsbury to help pay off her brother's debtors but he refused and overreacted to Bess's imagined provocations with uncalled-for hostility. There was now continuous friction between Bess and her husband and by 1579 reports of their discontent had reached court. Queen Elizabeth asked them to patch up their differences and although Bess tried, Shrewsbury only became meaner. He would explode into criticism and abuse of his wife with little or no provocation. The idyllic early years of the Shrewsbury marriage were over.

Bess became more pragmatic, and after long and heated discussions they eventually came to an agreement that Shrewsbury would be excused from paying what had been agreed in their 1567 marriage settlement if he returned to Bess all the land and property she had inherited from her third husband, William St Loe. It was mainly in Somerset and Gloucester but this at last gave Bess her financial independence. Although it was necessary for her to stay in the background, she controlled events through her protégés William and Charles Cavendish.

When James Hardwick died in debtor's prison in April 1581, Bess raised enough capital to purchase the Hardwick estate of her dead brother for £9,500. She was convinced that if the estate was managed well, it could produce a good return on the mineral reserves alone. Bess was a shrewd businesswoman and extremely competent. She acquired interests in land and mineral rights, and provided a much-used money-lending service to members of the nobility, dipping into the coffers stacked under her bed for loans at competitive rates.

But Shrewsbury was not a man of intellect, and argued that Bess had siphoned away his fortune into her own coffers. He started a vendetta against her and, although he'd agreed to return her property, he seized rents from the estates which he had returned to her, harried her tenants, and reacted to his wife's imagined provocations with renewed hostility.

On 21 January 1582, twenty-six-year-old Elizabeth Lennox died at Sheffield Manor, leaving her six-year-old daughter Arbella in the care of her grandmother Bess. That same year, Shrewsbury's son and heir Francis Talbot also died and his younger son Gilbert, married to Bess's daughter Mary, became Shrewsbury's heir.

Gilbert & Mary Talbot

Shrewsbury's finances and his gout were both troubling him deeply, and as trifling matters got blown out of proportion in his disturbed mind, his relationship with Bess cooled to frostiness. In order to retain her own sanity, Bess left him in Sheffield with Mary and returned to Chatsworth. At least there she had the freedom she had lacked as the Scottish queen's jailer. While his marriage was deteriorating – or possibly because of it – Shrewsbury discussed his problems with the Scottish Queen, but rumours were circulating that Shrewsbury and Mary were actually lovers and she had given birth to Shrewsbury's child. With Mary dropping hints of the catastrophic revelations she could make if she so wished, Bess sent many appeals to Shrewsbury to end the discourse between them, but he refused. He referred to Bess as 'his wicked and malicious wife, who was a woman of base parentage', and said he was ashamed of his choice of such a creature. Such harsh words cut Bess deeply, but Shrewsbury had become almost paranoid in his hatred of his once beloved wife.

7 Bess is Evicted from Chatsworth

It was inevitable that the rest of the family would be drawn into the incessant quarrels and disputes. Shrewsbury's son Gilbert Talbot, now heir to the earldom, tried to act as mediator between the battling elders but without success. Then, in the most bitter, underhanded act of all, Bess's own son and heir Henry Cavendish, who would inherit Chatsworth on Bess's death, decided to evict her. He teamed up with his stepfather and things came to a head in July 1584 when their men mounted an armed attack to forcibly take possession of Chatsworth. William Cavendish managed to hold off the attackers while Bess fled to Hardwick, where she took refuge in fear of her life.

She must have been devastated. For thirty years she had devoted all her money, time and energy into building Chatsworth. She had overseen every stage of the building, the landscaping and decor and now she was being forced to leave her beloved home by her own deceitful, scheming, Machiavellian son.

It was under this immense pressure that Bess surveyed the farmhouse and buildings at Hardwick that had grown piecemeal since Bess had lived there as a girl, with additions and repairs undertaken when money was available. It was damp and unwelcoming and not in a fit state to accommodate Bess and her household, having stood empty since her brother's death. She must have been at her lowest ebb when, in April 1584, she wrote to Sir Francis Walsingham, Queen Elizabeth's principal secretary (and notorious spymaster): *'For myself I hope to find some friend for meat and drink and so to end my life.'*

But Bess was a survivor, and with her independent income she rebuilt the old house to provide her with a roof over her head.

At last someone in authority realised that Shrewsbury could not continue to guard the Scottish Queen effectively on his own without Bess, and that autumn he received the news that Mary, Queen of Scots was to be moved away from the Shrewsbury household. In the course of sixteen years while Mary's fate hung in the balance, Shrewsbury had shunted his royal prisoner between his properties a total of forty-six times.

Queen Elizabeth signs Mary, Queen of Scots death warrant

iStock

This was the beginning of the end for Mary. Through his many agents, Walsingham mounted a new stage in his campaign to incriminate the Scottish Queen. He was looking for verification that it was too dangerous to keep her alive, and set about enmeshing her in what has become known as the Babington Plot. In June 1586 Mary wrote to Anthony Babington, approving a secret plan to assassinate Elizabeth and take her throne, and that sealed her fate. She was arrested, tried and convicted.

She was executed on 8 February 1587. It was exactly eighteen years after Mary had first arrived in Derbyshire to be placed in the care of the Earl and Countess of Shrewsbury.

Mary, Queen of Scots is lead to her execution

iStock

8 Bess Builds a New Hardwick Hall, fit for a Future Queen of England

The task of accommodating the captive queen had taken its toll on Shrewsbury's health, and he died on 18 November 1590, but this was a new beginning for Bess. Despite several quarrels with Gilbert Talbot, the new Earl of Shrewsbury, she finally gained possession of all the land and properties to which she was entitled under the marriage settlement. Her one regret must have been losing her beloved Chatsworth, but Bess was still full of vitality and ambition. She had rebuilt the Old Hardwick Hall, but now she began to build a new Hardwick Hall beside it.

Although the house was still unfinished, on 4 October 1597 Bess took up residence with her twenty-two-year-old granddaughter Arbella. It's believed the occasion was to mark her seventieth birthday. With her eye for business and practicality, Bess was a woman ahead of her time, an entrepreneur revelling in the challenge and rewards of her enterprise.

Bess of Hardwick, the local squire's daughter, had achieved so much, but now that she was settled in a home fit for a future queen she had an even greater ambition: to set her granddaughter on the throne of England. The death of Mary, Queen of Scots meant that Arbella was now joint next in line with her cousin James of Scotland, but because she was of royal blood only the Queen herself could select her marriage partner, and Elizabeth was in no hurry to do so. Arbella had been to court four times and the Queen had made the significant comment, 'Look at her well, for one day she will be even as I am', yet for the past thirteen years Arbella had been living with her aged grandmother, a virtual recluse at Hardwick.

Lady Arabella Stuart

In 1601 Bess enlisted Arbella's help to make an inventory of her possessions, along with a new will. She left the queen £200 to buy a cup of gold and sent a request for her to take Arbella back to court and find her a husband. The queen ignored the request, so, taking matters into her own hands, Arbella secretly approached Edward Seymour, the Earl of Hertford, regarding a marriage between herself and his grandson. They both had a strong claim to the English throne, but Seymour suspected something more devious and informed the authorities.

When Bess heard of her granddaughter's hare-brained scheme she begged the Queen to place her elsewhere or bestow her in marriage, but again the monarch took no action. Arbella even made plans to escape from Hardwick but the attempt was thwarted, and it was only when the Queen lay dying without naming her successor that it was decided to move Arbella to Wrest Park in Bedfordshire in case the succession was disputed and caused riots. When Queen Elizabeth died on 24 March 1603 and James VI of Scotland was proclaimed King James I of England, all Bess's dreams were shattered.

Arbella was invited to live at the royal court, where she was on friendly terms with her cousin James and his wife Anne. They asked Arbella to be godmother to their daughter Mary, the first royal christening in England since that of Edward VI in 1537. To mark the occasion James gave Arbella a blank patent for a peerage, and although loath to bequeath it to her uncle, William Cavendish, she gave way to pressure and he was granted the baronetcy of Hardwick.

In her advanced years, Bess purchased a site for her vault at the far end of the south altar of All Hallows Church in Derby (now Derby Cathedral). Her elaborate tomb, compatible with her station in life, was designed by Robert Smythson and included a life-size painted effigy. On 13 February 1608, Elizabeth, Countess of Shrewsbury died. Her body was embalmed, and she lay in state for three months while arrangements were made for her to be interred.

81 years Old.

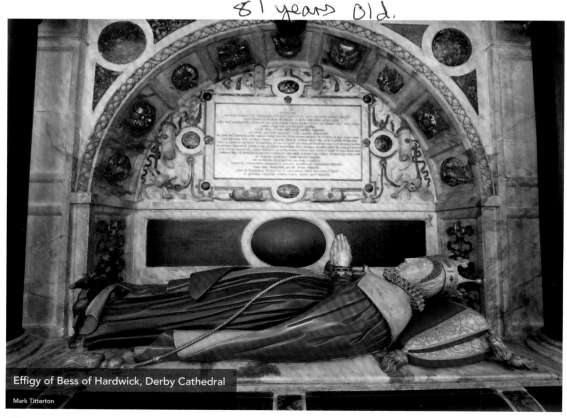

Effigy of Bess of Hardwick, Derby Cathedral

Mark Titterton

For details of other titles from Bradwell Books visit bradwellbooks.co.uk

NEW FOR 2018

Bradwells Book of The Peak District
ISBN 9781912060573

Colour the Peak District
ISBN 9781912060740

Bradwell's Images of
Derbyshire Blue John Stone
ISBN 9781912060641

Bradwell's Images of
Derbyshire Well Dressing
ISBN 9781912060658

Legends & Folklore the Peak District
ISBN 9781912060702

Walks for all Seasons Derbyshire
ISBN 9781912060528

AVAILABLE NOW

Derbyshire Dialect
ISBN 9781902674483

Derbyshire Ghost Stories
ISBN 9781902674629

Derbyshire Murder Stories
ISBN 9781909914285

Derbyshire Recipes
ISBN 9781902674858

Derbyshire Wit & Humour
ISBN 9781909914513

Bradwell's Family Cycle Rides:
The Peak District
ISBN 9781910551868

Bradwell's Images of the Peak District
ISBN 9781909914759

Bradwell's Longer Walks
in the Peak District
ISBN 9781910551677

Bradwell's Pocket Walking Guides
the Peak District
ISBN 9781910551936

Walks for All Ages Peak District
ISBN 9781909914018

Available from your local
bookshop or order online
bradwellbooks.co.uk